Born in 1926

By

Kerry Butters.

Born in 1926.

Millennium: 2nd millennium

Centuries: 19th century – **20th century** – 21st century

Decades: 1890s 1900s 1910s – **1920s** – 1930s 1940s 1950s

Years: 1923 1924 1925 – **1926** – 1927 1928 1929

1926 (MCMXXVI) was a common year starting on Friday (dominical letter C) of the Gregorian calendar and a common year starting on Thursday (dominical letter D) of the Julian calendar, the 1926th year of the Common Era (CE) and *Anno Domini* (AD) designations, the 926th year of the 2nd millennium, the 26th year of the 20th century, and the 7th year of the 1920s decade. Note that the Julian day for 1926 is 13 calendar days difference, which continued to be used from 1582 until the complete conversion of the Gregorian calendar was entirely done in 1929.

Contents

Events

January

- January 1
  - Flooding of the Rhine River struck Cologne; 50,000 were forced to evacuate their homes.
  - Ireland's first regular radio service, 2RN (later *Radio Éireann*), began broadcasting.
- January 3 – Theodoros Pangalos declared himself dictator in Greece.
- January 6 – The airline Deutsche Luft Hansa was founded in Berlin.
- January 8 – Abdul-Aziz ibn Saud was crowned King of Hejaz.
- January 12 – Freeman Gosden and Charles Correll premiered their radio program *Sam 'n' Henry*, in which the two white performers portray two black characters from Harlem looking to strike it rich in the big city. It was a precursor to Gosden and Correll's more popular later program, *Amos 'n' Andy*.

- January 16 – A BBC comic radio play broadcast by Ronald Knox about a workers' revolution caused a panic in London.
- January 21 – The Belgian Parliament accepted the Locarno Treaties.
- January 26 – Scottish inventor John Logie Baird demonstrated a mechanical television system for members of the Royal Institution and a reporter from *The Times* at his London laboratory.
- January 29 – Eugene O'Neill's *The Great God Brown* opened at the Greenwich Theatre.
- January 31 – British and Belgian troops left Cologne.

February

- February 1 – Land on Broadway and Wall Street in New York City was sold at a record $7 per sq inch.
- February 8 – Seán O'Casey's *The Plough and the Stars* opened at the Abbey Theatre in Dublin.
- February 9 – Flooding hit London suburbs.
- February 12 – The Irish minister for Justice, Kevin O'Higgins, appointed the Committee on Evil Literature.
- February 20 – The Berlin International Green Week debuted in Berlin.
- February 25 – Francisco Franco became General of Spain.

March

March 16: Goddard with rocket in 1926.

- March 6 – The Shakespeare Memorial Theatre in Stratford-upon-Avon was destroyed by fire.
- March 16 – Robert Goddard launched the first liquid-fuel rocket, at Auburn, Massachusetts.
- March 23 – Éamon de Valera organized Fianna Fáil in Ireland.

April

- April 4 – Greek dictator Theodoros Pangalos won the presidential election with 93.3% of the vote. Turnout was light as the result was considered a foregone conclusion.
- April 7 – An assassination attempt against Italian Fascist leader Benito Mussolini fails.
- April 12 – By a vote of 45–41, the United States Senate unseats Iowa Senator Smith W. Brookhart and seats Daniel F. Steck, after Brookhart had already served for over one year.
- April 17 – Zhang Zuolin's army captured Beijing.

- April 24 – Treaty of Berlin: Germany and the Soviet Union each pledged neutrality in the event of an attack on the other by a third party for the next five years.
- April 25 – Rezā Khan was crowned Shah of Iran under the name "Pahlevi".
- April 30 – African-American pilot Bessie Coleman was killed after falling 500 feet (150 m) from an airplane.

May

- May 3 – Coal miners were locked out in Britain.
- May 4 – The United Kingdom general strike began at midnight in support of the coal strike.
- May 9
  - Martial law was declared in Britain because of the general strike.
  - The French navy bombarded Damascus because of the Druze riots.
  - Explorer Richard E. Byrd and co-pilot Floyd Bennett claimed to be the first to fly over the North Pole in the *Josephine Ford* monoplane, taking off from Spitsbergen, Norway and returning 15 hours and 44 minutes later. Both men were immediately hailed as national heroes, though some experts have since been skeptical of the claim, believing that the plane was unlikely to have covered the entire distance and back in that short an amount of time. An entry in Byrd's diary discovered in 1996 suggested that the plane actually turned back 150 miles short of the North Pole due to an oil leak.
- May 10

- Talks between the government and strikers began in the U.K.
- Planes piloted by Major Harold Geiger and Horace Meek Hickam, students at the Air Corps Tactical School, collided in mid-air at Langley Field, Virginia. Hickam parachutes to safety.
- May 12
  - Roald Amundsen and his crew flew over the North Pole in the airship *Norge*.
  - UK General Strike 1926: In the United Kingdom, a general strike by trade unions ended (the strike began on May 3).
- May 12–May 14 – May Coup: Józef Piłsudski took over in Poland.
- May 18 – Evangelist Aimee Semple McPherson disappeared while visiting a Venice, California beach.
- May 20 – The United States Congress passed the Air Commerce Act, licensing pilots and planes.
- May 23 – The first Lebanese constitution was established.
- May 26 – The Rif War ended when Rif rebels surrendered in Morocco.
- May 28 – The 1926 coup d'état commanded by Manuel Gomes da Costa in Portugal installed the Ditadura Nacional (National Dictatorship), followed by António de Oliveira Salazar's Estado Novo.

June

- June 4 – Ignacy Mościcki became president of Poland.

- June 7 The Liberal politician Carl Gustaf Ekman succeeds Rickard Sandler as Prime Minister of Sweden .
- June 19 – DeFord Bailey was the first African-American to perform on Nashville's Grand Ole Opry.
- June 29 – Arthur Meighen briefly returned to office as Prime Minister of Canada during the King-Byng Affair.

July

- July 1 – The Mammoth Cave National Park is authorized by the United States Congress.
- July 1 – The Kuomintang began a military unification campaign in northern China.
- July 3 – A Caudron C.61 aircraft operated by Compagnie Internationale de Navigation Aérienne crashed in Czechoslovakia.
- July 9 – General Óscar Carmona took power in a military coup in Portugal.
- July 10 – A bolt of lightning struck Picatinny Arsenal in New Jersey. The resulting fire caused several million pounds of explosives to blow up in the next two to three days.
- July 15 – BEST buses made their début in Bombay.
- July 23 – Fox Film bought the patents of the Movietone sound system for recording sound onto film.
- July 26 – The National Bar Association incorporated in the United States.

August

- August 1 – In Mexico, the entry into force of anticlerical measures stipulated in the constitution of 1917 caused the Cristero War.
- August 6
    - Gertrude Ederle became the first woman to swim the English Channel from France to England.
    - In New York, the Warner Brothers' Vitaphone system premiered with the movie *Don Juan* starring John Barrymore.
- August 18
    - The British miners' union began negotiations with the government.
    - A weather map was televised for the first time, sent from NAA Arlington to the Weather Bureau office in Washington, D.C.
- August 22 – In Greece, Georgios Kondylis ousted Theodoros Pangalos.
- August 23 – The sudden death of popular Hollywood actor and sex symbol Rudolph Valentino at the age of only 31 years old caused mass grief and hysteria around the world.
- August 25 – Pavlos Kountouriotis announced that dictatorship had ended in Greece and he was now the president.

September

- September 1 – Lebanon under the French Mandate got its first constitution, thereby becoming a republic. Charles Debbas was elected president.
- September 8 – The German Weimar Republic joined the League of Nations.
- September 11
    - Aloha Tower was officially dedicated at Honolulu Harbor in the Territory of Hawai'i.
    - In Rome, Italy, Gino Lucetti threw a bomb at Benito Mussolini's car, but Mussolini was unhurt.
- September 14 – The Locarno Treaties of 1925 were ratified in Geneva and came into effect.
- September 16 – Philip Dunning and George Abbott's play *Broadway* premieres in New York City.
- September 18 – Great Miami Hurricane: A strong hurricane devastated Miami, leaving over 100 dead and causing several hundred million dollars in damage (equal to nearly $100 billion today).
- September 20 – The North Side Gang attempted to assassinate Al Capone, spraying his headquarters in Cicero, Illinois with over a thousand rounds of machine gun fire in broad daylight as Capone was eating there. Capone escaped harm.
- September 21 – French war ace René Fonck and three others attempted to fly the Atlantic in pursuit of the Orteig Prize. Before the newsreel cameras at Roosevelt Field New York, the modified Sikorsky S-35 crashes on take-off and bursts into flames. Fonck survived but two of his men are killed.

- September 23 – Gene Tunney defeated Jack Dempsey and became heavyweight boxing champion of the world.
- September 25
    - The League of Nations Slavery Convention abolished all types of slavery.
    - William Lyon Mackenzie King returned to office as Prime Minister of Canada after winning the Canadian federal election.

October

- October 2 – Józef Piłsudski became prime minister of Poland.
- October 12 – British miners agreed to end their strike.
- October 14 – A. A. Milne's children's book *Winnie-the-Pooh* was published in London, featuring the eponymous bear.
- October 19 – The 1926 Imperial Conference opened in London.
- October 20 – A hurricane killed 650 in Cuba.
- October 23
    - Leon Trotsky and Lev Kamenev were removed from the Politburo of the Central Committee of the Communist Party of the Soviet Union.
    - A decree in Italy banned women from holding public office.
    - The Fazal Mosque, the first purpose-built in London and the first Ahmadiyya mosque in Britain, is completed.
- October 31 – Magician Harry Houdini died of gangrene and peritonitis that has developed after his appendix ruptured.

November

- November 5 – The APOEL FC is founded.
- November 10 – In San Francisco, a necrophiliac serial killer named Earle Nelson (dubbed "Gorilla Man") killed and then rapes his 9th victim, a boarding house landlady named Mrs. William Edmonds.
- November 11 – The United States Numbered Highway System, including U.S. Route 66, was established.
- November 15
    - The *NBC* radio network opened with 24 stations (formed by Westinghouse, General Electric and RCA).
    - The Balfour Declaration was approved by the 1926 Imperial Conference, making the Commonwealth dominions equal and independent.
- November 24
    - The village of Rocquebillier in the French Riviera was almost destroyed in a massive hailstorm.
    - Sri Aurobindo retired, leaving *The Mother* to run the Sri Aurobindo Ashram in Puducherry, India.
- November 25 – The death penalty was re-established in Italy.
- November 26 – All Italian Communist deputies were arrested.
- November 27 – The restoration of Colonial Williamsburg began in Williamsburg, Virginia.

December

- December 2 – British prime minister Stanley Baldwin ended the martial law that had been declared due to general strike.
- December 3 – Agatha Christie disappeared from her home in Surrey; on December 14 she was found at a Harrogate hotel.
- December 7 – The Council for the Preservation of Rural England (CPRE) founded; now the Campaign to Protect Rural England.
- December 17 – 1926 Lithuanian coup d'état: A democratically elected government was overthrown in Lithuania; Antanas Smetona assumed power.
- December 18 – Turkey converted to the Gregorian calendar, making the next day January 1 1927.
- December 23 – Nicaraguan President Adolfo Díaz requested U.S. military assistance in the ongoing civil war. American peacekeeping troops immediately set up neutral zones in Puerto Cabezas and at the mouth of the Rio Grande to protect American and foreign lives and property.
- December 26 – In the history of Japan, the Shōwa period began from this day due to the death of Emperor Taishō on the day before. His son Hirohito reigned as Emperor of Japan until 1989.

Date unknown

- Dr. Muthulakshmi Reddi became the first woman appointed to a legislature in India, the Madras Legislative Council.
- Stephen H. Langdon began excavations in Jemdet Nasr finding proto-cuneiform clay tablets (3100–2900 BCE)

- Phencyclidine *(PCP, angel dust)* was first synthesized.
- Widows' pensions were introduced in New South Wales, Australia.
- The short-lived Western Australian Secession League was founded.
- Earl W. Bascom, rodeo cowboy and artist, designed and marked rodeo's first high-cut rodeo chaps at Stirling, Alberta Canada.
- The International African Institute is founded in London.
- Raymond Pearl published his landmark book, *Alcohol and Longevity*.
- American microbiologist Selman Waksman published *Enzymes*.
- The Pike School of Andover, Massachusetts was founded.
- Industrial output surpassed the level of 1913 in the USSR.
- Al Capone was at the apex of his power.

Births

January

- January 1 – Claudio Villa, Italian singer (d. 1987)
- January 2 – Harold Bradley, American session guitarist on country music records
- January 3
  - Felicitas Kuhn, Austrian illustrator
  - George Martin, English producer of *The Beatles* (d. 2016)
- January 5 – William De Witt Snodgrass, American poet (d. 2009)
- January 6

- Mickey Hargitay, Hungarian actor and bodybuilder (d. 2006)
- January 8
  - Chester Feldman, American television game show producer (d. 1997)
  - Evelyn Lear, American soprano (d. 2012)
  - Hanae Mori, Japanese fashion designer
  - Soupy Sales, American comedian (d. 2009)
- January 11 – Lev Dyomin, cosmonaut (d. 1998)
- January 12 – Ray Price, American singer (d. 2013)
- January 14 – Tom Tryon, American actor and novelist (d. 1991)
- January 15 – Maria Schell, Austrian actress (d. 2005)
- January 17 – Moira Shearer, Scottish actress and dancer (d. 2006)
- January 19 – Fritz Weaver, American actor
- January 20
  - Patricia Neal, American actress (*The Day The Earth Stood Still*) (d. 2010)
  - David Tudor, American pianist and composer (d. 1996)
- January 21 – Steve Reeves, American actor (d. 2000)
- January 23 – Bal Thackeray, Indian politician (d. 2012)
- January 26 – Franco Evangelisti, Italian composer (d. 1980)
- January 27
  - Fritz Spiegl, Austrian journalist (d. 2003)
  - Ingrid Thulin, Swedish actress (d. 2004)
- January 29 – Abdus Salam, Pakistani physicist, Nobel Prize laureate (d. 1996)

February

Valéry Giscard d'Estaing

Leslie Nielsen

- February 2
  - Valéry Giscard d'Estaing, President of France
  - Miguel Obando y Bravo, Nicaraguan Roman Catholic prelate, archbishop of Managua and cardinal
- February 3 – Hans-Jochen Vogel, German politician
- February 4 – Gyula Grosics, Hungarian footballer (d. 2014)
- February 7
  - Konstantin Feoktistov, Soviet cosmonaut (d. 2009)
  - Bill Hoest, American cartoonist (d. 1988)
- February 8 – Neal Cassady, American writer (d. 1968)
- February 10 – Danny Blanchflower, Northern Irish footballer and football manager (d. 1993)

- February 11
    - Paul Bocuse, French chef
    - Alexander Gibson, British conductor and founder of the Scottish Opera (d. 1995)
    - Leslie Nielsen, Canadian-American actor (d. 2010)
- February 14 – Al Brodax, American film and television producer
- February 16
    - Margot Frank, sister of Anne Frank (d. 1945)
    - John Schlesinger, British film director (d. 2003)
- February 17 – John Meyendorff, Orthodox scholar, protopresbiter, and educator (d. 1992)
- February 20
    - Whitney Blake, American actress (d. 2002)
    - Richard Matheson, American author (d. 2013)
    - Bob Richards, American track and field athlete
- February 22 – Kenneth Williams, English actor (d. 1988)
- February 24 – Dave Sands, Australian boxer (d. 1952)
- February 26 – Verne Gagne, American professional wrestler (d. 2015)
- February 27 – David H. Hubel, Canadian neuroscientist, recipient of the Nobel Prize in Physiology or Medicine (d. 2013)
- February 28 – Svetlana Alliluyeva, Russian author (d. 2011)

March

Andrzej Wajda

Jerry Lewis

Siegfried Lenz

- March 1
  - Pete Rozelle, American commissioner of the National Football League (d. 1996)
  - Robert Clary, French-American actor, author and lecturer

- March 2 – Murray Rothbard, American economist (d. 1995)
- March 3 – James Merrill, American poet (d. 1995)
- March 4
    - Richard DeVos, American billionaire, co-founder of *Amway*
    - James J. Eagan, former Mayor of Florissant, Missouri (d. 2000)
    - Fran Warren, American popular singer (d. 2013)
- March 6
    - Alan Greenspan, American economist and former Chairman of the Federal Reserve
    - Andrzej Wajda, Polish film director
- March 8 – Sultan Salahuddin of Selangor (d. 2001)
- March 11
    - Derek Benfield, English playwright and actor (d. 2009)
    - Thomas Starzl, American physician
- March 13 – Carlos Roberto Reina, President of Honduras (d. 2003)
- March 15 – Norm Van Brocklin, American football player (d. 1983)
- March 16
    - Charles Goodell, American politician (d. 1987)
    - Jerry Lewis, American comedian and humanitarian (*Muscular Dystrophy Telethon*)
- March 17
    - Jaynne Bittner, American female baseball player
    - Siegfried Lenz, German writer (d. 2014)
- March 18 – Peter Graves, American actor (d. 2010)
- March 24
    - Dario Fo, Italian author, Nobel Prize laureate

- Ventsislav Yankov, Bulgarian pianist
- March 25
  - László Papp, Hungarian boxer (d. 2003)
  - Gene Shalit, American film critic and television personality
- March 28 – Cayetana Fitz-James Stuart, 18th Duchess of Alba, Spanish aristocrat (d. 2014)
- March 30
  - Ingvar Kamprad, Swedish businessman
  - Peter Marshall, American singer and television host (*Hollywood Squares*)
- March 31 – John Fowles, English writer (d. 2005)

April

Hugh Hefner

Elizabeth II

Cloris Leachman

Harper Lee

- April 1
  - Charles Bressler, American tenor (d. 1996)
  - Anne McCaffrey, American author (d. 2011)
- April 2
  - Jack Brabham, Australian race car driver (d. 2014)
  - Robert Holmes, British scriptwriter (d. 1986)
- April 3
  - Gus Grissom, American astronaut (d. 1967)
  - R.W. Schambach, American televangelist (d. 2012)
- April 6
  - Sergio Franchi, Italian tenor and actor (d. 1990)
  - Gil Kane, Latvian-born cartoonist (d. 2000)
  - Ian Paisley, Northern Irish politician (d. 2014)
- April 7

- o Prem Nazir, Indian actor (d. 1989)
- o Miyoko Asō, Japanese voice actress
- April 9 – Hugh Hefner, American magazine editor (*Playboy*)
- April 12
  - o Khozh-Akhmed Bersanov, Chechen ethnographer
  - o Jane Withers, American actress
- April 14
  - o Frank Daniel, Czech-born writer, producer, director, teacher (d. 1996)
  - o George Robledo, Chilean soccer player (d. 1989)
  - o Leopoldo Calvo-Sotelo, Spanish politician (d. 2008)
- April 17 – Gerry McNeil, Canadian hockey player (d. 2004)
- April 19 – Rawya Ateya, Egyptian politician and first female parliamentarian in the Arab world (d. 1997)
- April 21
  - o Elizabeth II, Queen of the United Kingdom
  - o Arthur Rowley, English footballer (d. 2002)
- April 22
  - o Charlotte Rae, American actress and singer
  - o James Stirling, Scottish architect (d. 1992)
- April 24 – Thorbjörn Fälldin, Prime Minister of Sweden
- April 25 – Gertrude Fröhlich-Sandner, Austrian politician (d. 2008)
- April 26
  - o David Coleman, British TV sports broadcaster (d. 2013)
  - o Michael Mathias Prechtl, German illustrator (d. 2003)
- April 27 – Tim LaHaye, American evangelist, speaker and author
- April 28 – Harper Lee, American novelist (d. 2016)
- April 29 – Paul Baran, American internet pioneer (d. 2011)

- April 30
  - Edmund Cooper, British author and poet (d. 1982)
  - Cloris Leachman, American actress

May

David Attenborough

Don Rickles

Dietmar Schönherr

- May 5
  - Ann B. Davis, American actress (*The Brady Bunch*) (d. 2014)
  - Bing Russell, American actor (d. 2003)
- May 8

- Sir David Attenborough, British broadcaster, naturalist and producer
- Don Rickles, American comedian and actor
- May 10 – Tichi Wilkerson Kassel, American film personality and publisher of *The Hollywood Reporter* (d. 2004)
- May 14 – Eric Morecambe, English comedian and author (d. 1984)
- May 15
  - Anthony Shaffer, English novelist and playwright (d. 2001), twin brother of:
  - Peter Shaffer, English playwright
- May 17 – Franz Sondheimer, German-born British chemist (d. 1981)
- May 17 – Dietmar Schönherr, Austrian film actor (d. 2014)
- May 18 – Dirch Passer, Danish actor (d. 1980)
- May 20 – John Lucarotti, TV writer (d. 1994)
- May 21 – Robert Creeley, American Poet (d. 2005)
- May 25 – Bill Sharman, American basketball player and coach (d. 2013)
- May 26 – Miles Davis, American musician (d. 1991)
- May 27 – Kees Rijvers, Dutch football player and manager
- May 29 – Abdoulaye Wade, President of Senegal
- May 30
  - Johnny Gimble, American country musician and fiddler (d. 2015)
  - Tsuneo Watanabe, Japanese businessman

June

Marilyn Monroe

Mel Brooks

- June 1
  - Andy Griffith, American actor (d. 2012)
  - Marilyn Monroe, American actress (d. 1962)
- June 3
  - Roscoe Bartlett, Republican member of the United States House of Representatives
  - Allen Ginsberg, American poet (*Howl*) (d. 1997)
- June 6 – Klaus Tennstedt, German conductor (d. 1998)
- June 9 – Happy Rockefeller, American socialite (d. 2015)
- June 10 – Lionel Jeffries, British film director and actor (d. 2010)
- June 11 – Frank Plicka, Czech-born photographer (d. 2010)

- June 12 – Gaspare di Mercurio, Italian doctor and author (d. 2001)
- June 13 – Paul Lynde, American comedian (d. 1982)
- June 15 – Shigeru Kayano, Japanese Ainu activist (d. 2006)
- June 16 – William F. Roemer, Jr., United States FBI agent (d. 1996)
- June 18 – Allan Sandage, American astronomer (d. 2010)
- June 21 – Conrad Hall, Tahitian-born cinematographer (d. 2003)
- June 22 – Tadeusz Konwicki, Polish filmmaker (d. 2015)
- June 25 – Ingeborg Bachmann, Austrian writer (d. 1973)
- June 28 – Mel Brooks, American entertainer (*The Producers*)
- June 29 – Jaber Al-Ahmad Al-Jaber Al-Sabah, Emir of Kuwait (d. 2006)
- June 30 – Paul Berg, American chemist, Nobel Prize laureate
- June 30 – Peter Alexander, Austrian actor, singer and entertainer (d. 2011)

July

Alfredo Di Stéfano

- July 1
  - Robert Fogel, American economist, Nobel Prize laureate (d. 2013)

- Carl Hahn, German automotive executive, chairman of Volkswagen from 1982 to 1993
  - Hans Werner Henze, German composer (d. 2012)
- July 4
  - Alfredo Di Stéfano, Argentine-born footballer (d. 2014)
  - Amos Elon, Israeli writer (d. 2009)
  - Mary Stuart, American soap actress (d. 2002)
- July 8 – Elisabeth Kübler-Ross, Swiss-born psychiatrist (d. 2004)
- July 9 – Ben Roy Mottelson, American-born physicist, Nobel Prize laureate
- July 10 – Fred Gwynne, American actor and author (d. 1993)
- July 11 – Joe Houston, American saxophonist (d. 2015)
- July 14 – Harry Dean Stanton, American film and television actor
- July 15
  - Leopoldo Galtieri, Argentine dictator (d. 2003)
  - Raymond Gosling, English physicist (d. 2015)
- July 16
  - Stanley Clements, American actor (d. 1981)
  - Irwin Rose, American biologist, recipient of the Nobel Prize in Chemistry (d. 2015)
- July 17 – William Pierson, American television, motion picture and stage actor (d. 2004)
- July 18
  - Robert Sloman, English writer (d. 2005)
  - Joshua Fishman, American linguist (d. 2015)
- July 19 – Helen Gallagher, American actress, dancer, singer, and makeup artist

- July 24 – Hans Günter Winkler, German equestrian and show jumper
- July 26
    - James Best, American actor (*The Dukes of Hazzard*) (d. 2015)
    - Lennox Sebe, President of Ciskei bantustan (d. 1994)
- July 27 – Doris Satterfield, American professional baseball player (d. 1993)
- July 28 – Walt Brown, American presidential candidate
- July 30 – Sir Patrick Russell QC, PC, British High Court Judge (d. 2002)
- July 31 – Hilary Putnam, American philosopher, mathematician and computer scientist (d. 2016)

August

Tony Bennett

Fidel Castro

René Goscinny

Jiang Zemin

- August 1 – Hannah Hauxwell, English TV personality
- August 2 – Sy Mah, Canadian marathoner (d. 1988)
- August 3
  - Tony Bennett, American singer ("I Left My Heart in San Francisco")
  - Anthony Sampson, British journalist and biographer (d. 2004)
- August 6 – Norman Wexler, Academy Award nominated Screenwriter (d. 1999)
- August 7 – Stan Freberg, American author, recording artist and comedian (d. 2015)
- August 11
  - Claus von Bülow, Danish-born British socialite

- Aaron Klug, Lithuanian-born chemist, Nobel Prize laureate
- August 12
  - John Derek, American actor and director (d. 1998)
  - Hiroshi Koizumi, Japanese actor (d. 2015)
  - Wallace Markfield, American writer (d. 2002)
- August 13 – Fidel Castro, Cuban revolutionary and politician
- August 14 – René Goscinny, French comic book writer (d. 1977)
- August 15 – Konstantinos Stephanopoulos, former President of Greece
- August 17 – Jiang Zemin, former General Secretary of the Communist Party of China and President of the People's Republic of China
- August 19
  - Angus Scrimm, American actor (d. 2016)
  - Arthur Rock, American venture capitalist
- August 23 – Clifford Geertz, American anthropologist (d. 2006)
- August 26 – Robert Vickrey, American artist and author (d. 2011)
- August 27 – Pat Coombs, British actress (d. 2002)
- August 29 – Betty Lynn, American actress

September

James Lipton

- September 2 – Ibrahim Nasir Rannabanderyi Kilegefan, Maldivian president (d. 2008)
- September 3
    - Uttam Kumar, Bengali actor (d. 1980)
    - Irene Papas, Greek actress and singer
- September 6
    - Claus van Amsberg, German born Prince Consort of the Netherlands (d. 2002)
    - Maurice Cowling, British historian (d. 2005)
    - Maurice Prather, American photographer (d. 2001)
- September 7
    - Ronnie Gilbert, American folk singer and songwriter (d. 2015)
    - Don Messick, American voice actor (d. 1997)
- September 8 – Sergio Pininfarina, Italian automobile designer (d. 2012)
- September 14 – Dick Dale, American singer and musician (d. 2014)
- September 15 – Jean-Pierre Serre, French mathematician
- September 16

- John Knowles, American author (d. 2001)
- Robert H. Schuller, American televangelist, motivational speaker and author (d. 2015)
- Raymond Barnes, The best great grandfather ever (d. 2016)

- September 19
  - Masatoshi Koshiba, Japanese physicist, Nobel Prize laureate
  - James Lipton, American television personality and writer
  - Duke Snider, American baseball player (d. 2011)
- September 21
  - Donald A. Glaser, American physicist, Nobel Prize laureate (d. 2013)
  - Noor Jehan, Pakistani singer and actress (d. 2000)
- September 23 – John Coltrane, American jazz saxophonist (d. 1967)
- September 24 – Aubrey Burl, British archaeologist
- September 26 – Julie London, American actress and singer (d. 2000)
- September 28 – Jerry Clower, American country comedian (d. 1998)
- September 30
  - Robin Roberts, American baseball player (d. 2010)
  - Dave Hunt, American apologist, speaker, radio commentator and author (d. 2013)

October

Chuck Berry

- October 4 – Senaida Wirth, American female professional baseball player (d. 1967)
- October 7 – Czesław Ryll-Nardzewski, Polish mathematician (d. 2015)
- October 9 – Ruth Ellis, British murderess (d. 1955)
- October 13
  - Jesse L. Brown, first African-American aviator in the United States Navy (d. 1950)
  - Kazuo Nakamura, Japanese-Canadian painter, part of the Painters Eleven (d. 2002)
- October 15
  - Michel Foucault, French philosopher (d. 1984)
  - Jean Peters, American actress (d. 2000)
  - Karl Richter, German conductor (d. 1981)
- October 17
  - Julie Adams, American actress
  - Beverly Garland, American actress and businesswoman (d. 2008)
- October 18
  - Chuck Berry, American singer-songwriter and guitarist
  - Klaus Kinski, German actor (d. 1991)

- Pauline Pirok, American female professional baseball player
- October 21 – Bob Rosburg, American golfer (d. 2009)
- October 22 – Gloria Carter Spann, sister of former President Jimmy Carter (d. 1990)
- October 25 – Galina Vishnevskaya, Russian soprano (d. 2012)
- October 28 – Bowie Kuhn, American Commissioner of Baseball (d. 2007)
- October 29
  - Necmettin Erbakan, 25th Prime Minister of Turkey (d. 2011)
  - Jon Vickers, Canadian operatic tenor (d. 2015)
- October 30 – Lois Wyse, American advertising executive, author and columnist (d. 2007)
- October 31 – Jimmy Savile, English DJ and television presenter (d. 2011)

November

- November 1 – Betsy Palmer, American actress (d. 2015)
- November 3 – Valdas Adamkus, President of Lithuania
- November 5 – John Berger, English art critic, novelist and painter
- November 6 – Frank Carson, Northern Irish comedian (d. 2012)
- November 7 – Dame Joan Sutherland, Australian soprano (d. 2010)
- November 11 – Maria Teresa de Filippis, Italian automobile racing driver (d. 2016)
- November 15 – Helmut Fischer, German actor (d. 1997)

- November 16 – Amy Applegren, American professional baseball player (d. 2011)
- November 16 – Ton de Leeuw, Dutch composer (d. 1996)
- November 19 – Jeane Kirkpatrick, American ambassador (d. 2006)
- November 20 – John Gardner, English spy novelist (d. 2007)
- November 23
    - Sathya Sai Baba, Indian spiritual leader (d. 2011)
    - R. L. Burnside, American musician (d. 2005)
- November 24 – Tsung-Dao Lee, Chinese physicist, Nobel Prize laureate
- November 25 – Poul Anderson, American science fiction author (d. 2001)
- November 26 – Peter van Pels, German-Dutch love interest of Anne Frank (d. 1945)
- November 30
    - Richard Crenna, American actor (d. 2003)
    - Andrew Schally, Polish-born American endocrinologist, recipient of the Nobel Prize in Physiology or Medicine

December

- December 1
    - Allyn Ann McLerie, Canadian-American actress and dancer
    - Robert Symonds, American actor (d. 2007)
- December 9 – Henry Way Kendall, American physicist, Nobel Prize laureate (d. 1999)
- December 13 – George Rhoden, Jamaican athlete

- December 16 – James McCracken, American tenor (d. 1988)
- December 17
  - Allan V. Cox, American geologist (d. 1987)
  - Bill Keightley, American equipment manager for the University of Kentucky men's basketball team from 1962 to 2008 (d. 2008)
- December 20
  - Geoffrey Howe, British politician (d. 2015)
  - Otto Graf Lambsdorff, German politician (d. 2009)
  - David Levine, U.S. caricaturist (d. 2009)
- December 21
  - Joe Paterno, American football coach and philanthropist (d. 2012)
  - Elisabeth Elliot, American Christian author and speaker (d. 2015)
- December 22 – Alcides Ghiggia, Uruguayan footballer (d. 2015)
- December 23 – Robert Bly, American poet
- December 26 – Gina Pellón, Cuban painter (d. 2014)

Deaths

January–March

Camillo Golgi

Heike Kamerlingh Onnes

Antoni Gaudi

- Billy Snedden, Australian politician (d. 1987)

- January 4 – Margherita of Savoy, queen consort of Italy (b. 1851)
- January 15 – Louis Majorelle, French furniture designer (b. 1859)
- January 21 – Camillo Golgi, Italian physician, recipient of the Nobel Prize in Physiology or Medicine (b. 1843)
- January 28
    ○ Katō Takaaki, 24th Prime Minister of Japan (b. 1860)
    ○ Ernest Troubridge, British admiral (b. 1862)
- January 30 – Barbara La Marr, American film actress (b. 1896)
- February 6 – Carrie Clark Ward, stage and film character actress (b. 1862)

- February 8 – William Bateson, English geneticist (b. 1861)
- February 21 – Heike Kamerlingh Onnes, Dutch physicist, Nobel Prize laureate (b. 1853)
- February 24
    - John Jacob Bausch, German-American optician who co-founded Bausch & Lomb (b. 1830)
    - Eddie Plank, American baseball player and MLB Hall of Famer (b. 1875)
- March 11 – Usui Mikao, Japanese founder of Reiki (b. 1865)
- March 12 – E. W. Scripps, American newspaper publisher (b. 1854)
- March 16 – Sergeant Stubby, World War I American hero war dog.
- March 17 – Aleksei Brusilov, Russian general (b. 1853)
- March 24 – Sizzo, Prince of Schwarzburg (b. 1860)
- March 26 – Constantin Fehrenbach, former Chancellor of Germany (b. 1852)

April–June

- April 1 – Jacob Pavlovich Adler, Russian actor (b. 1855)
- April 9 – Henry Miller, English-born American stage actor and producer (b. 1859)
- April 10 – Ōshima Yoshimasa, Japanese general (b. 1850)
- April 20 – Billy Quirk, American actor (b. 1873)
- April 24 – Sunjong, last Emperor of Korea (b. 1874)
- April 25 – Ellen Key, Swedish feminist writer (b. 1849)
- April 28 – Kawamura Kageaki, Japanese field marshal (b. 1850)
- April 30 – Bessie Coleman, African-American pilot (b. 1892)

- May 9 – J. M. Dent, British publisher (b. 1849)
- May 16 – Mehmed VI, last Ottoman Sultan (b. 1861)
- May 26 – Symon Petliura, Ukrainian independence fighter (b. 1879)
- June 8 – Emily Hobhouse, British welfare campaigner (b. 1860)
- June 9 – Sanford B. Dole, President of Hawaii and 1st Territorial Governor of Hawaii (b. 1844)
- June 10 – Antoni Gaudí, Catalan architect (b. 1852)
- June 14 – Mary Cassatt, American artist (b. 1844)

July–September

- July 2 – Émile Coué, French psychologist (b. 1857)
- July 12
  - Gertrude Bell, English archaeologist, writer, spy, and administrator; known as the "Uncrowned Queen of Iraq" (b. 1868)
  - John W. Weeks, American politician in the Republican Party (b. 1860)
- July 22
  - Willard Louis, American actor (b. 1882)
  - Friedrich von Wieser, Austrian economist (b. 1851)
- July 26 – Robert Todd Lincoln, American statesman and businessman, son of 16th President Abraham Lincoln (b. 1843)
- August 14 – John H. Moffitt, American politician (b. 1843)
- August 21 – Ugyen Wangchuck, King of Bhutan (b. 1861)
- August 22 – Charles W. Eliot, President of Harvard University (b. 1834)

- August 23 – Rudolph Valentino, Italian actor (b. 1895)
- August 27 – John Rodgers, American naval officer and naval aviation pioneer (b. 1881)
- August 30 – Eddie Lyons, American actor (b. 1886)
- September 15 – Rudolf Christoph Eucken, German writer, Nobel Prize laureate (b. 1846)
- September 21 – Léon Charles Thévenin, French telegraph engineer (b. 1857)
- September 25 – Herbert Booth, third son of William and Catherine Booth (b. 1862)

October–December

Claude Monet

Emperor Taishō

- October 7 – Emil Kraepelin, German psychiatrist (b. 1856)
- October 9 – Josias von Heeringen, German general (b. 1850)

- October 11 – Hymie Weiss, American gangster (b. 1898)
- October 16 – Princess Frederica of Hanover (b. 1848)
- October 19 – Victor Babeş, Romanian bacteriologist (b. 1854)
- October 20 – Eugene V. Debs, American labor and political leader (b. 1855)
- October 31
    - Harry Houdini, Hungarian-born escapologist (b. 1874)
    - Charles Vance Millar, Canadian businessman (b. 1853)
- November 3 – Annie Oakley, American sharpshooter and entertainer (b. 1860)
- November 7 – Tom Forman, American actor and director (b. 1893)
- December 2 – Gérard Cooreman, former Prime Minister of Belgium (b. 1852)
- December 4 – Ivana Kobilca, Slovenian painter (b. 1861)
- December 5 – Claude Monet, French painter (b. 1840)
- December 10 – Nikola Pašić, Serbian and Yugoslav statesman, several times Prime Minister (b. 1855)
- December 16 – William Larned, American tennis champion (b. 1872)
- December 17 – Lars Magnus Ericsson, Swedish inventor and founder of Ericsson (b. 1846)
- December 22 – Mina Arndt, New Zealander painter (b. 1885)
- December 24 – Johan Castberg, Norwegian Radical politician (b. 1862)
- December 25 – Emperor Taishō, 123rd Emperor of Japan (b. 1879)
- December 28 – Robert Felkin, British writer (b. 1853)
- December 29 – Rainer Maria Rilke, Austrian poet (b. 1875)

Nobel Prizes

- Physics – Jean Baptiste Perrin
- Chemistry – Theodor Svedberg
- Physiology or Medicine – Johannes Andreas Grib Fibiger
- Literature – Grazia Deledda
- Peace – Aristide Briand, Gustav Stresemann

In the News.

Winnie-the-Pooh is published by Author A. A. Milne.

On January 27th John Logie Baird conducts the first public demonstration of a television.

Gertrude "Trudy" Ederle became the first woman to swim the English Channel.

Hirohito is crowned emperor of Japan.

Escape artist and famous entertainer Harry Houdini dies at the age of 52.

U.S. Route 66 is created and runs from Chicago to Los Angeles.

Silent film heart throb Rudolph Valentino dies <u>August 23rd</u> causing a worldwide frenzy among his fans.

General strike in England begins in support of the coal miners strike on <u>May 3rd</u> and ends May 12th.

Inventions, Liquid Fuel Rocket and Aerosol Sprays.

Ford announces the 40-hour week.

Actress Greta Garbo makes her American film debut in "Torrent."

Population: US 115 million, Britain 45 million.

1926 Calender.

January 1926
Sun	Mon	Tue	Wed	Thu	Fri	Sat
					1	2
3	4	5	6	7	8	9
10	11	12	13	14	15	16
17	18	19	20	21	22	23
24	25	26	27	28	29	30
31						

February 1926
Sun	Mon	Tue	Wed	Thu	Fri	Sat
	1	2	3	4	5	6
7	8	9	10	11	12	13
14	15	16	17	18	19	20
21	22	23	24	25	26	27
28						

March 1926
Sun	Mon	Tue	Wed	Thu	Fri	Sat
	1	2	3	4	5	6
7	8	9	10	11	12	13
14	15	16	17	18	19	20
21	22	23	24	25	26	27
28	29	30	31			

April 1926
Sun	Mon	Tue	Wed	Thu	Fri	Sat
				1	2	3
4	5	6	7	8	9	10
11	12	13	14	15	16	17
18	19	20	21	22	23	24
25	26	27	28	29	30	

May 1926
Sun	Mon	Tue	Wed	Thu	Fri	Sat
						1
2	3	4	5	6	7	8
9	10	11	12	13	14	15
16	17	18	19	20	21	22
23	24	25	26	27	28	29
30	31					

June 1926
Sun	Mon	Tue	Wed	Thu	Fri	Sat
		1	2	3	4	5
6	7	8	9	10	11	12
13	14	15	16	17	18	19
20	21	22	23	24	25	26
27	28	29	30			

July 1926
Sun	Mon	Tue	Wed	Thu	Fri	Sat
				1	2	3
4	5	6	7	8	9	10
11	12	13	14	15	16	17
18	19	20	21	22	23	24
25	26	27	28	29	30	31

August 1926
Sun	Mon	Tue	Wed	Thu	Fri	Sat
1	2	3	4	5	6	7
8	9	10	11	12	13	14
15	16	17	18	19	20	21
22	23	24	25	26	27	28
29	30	31				

September 1926
Sun	Mon	Tue	Wed	Thu	Fri	Sat
			1	2	3	4
5	6	7	8	9	10	11
12	13	14	15	16	17	18
19	20	21	22	23	24	25
26	27	28	29	30		

October 1926
Sun	Mon	Tue	Wed	Thu	Fri	Sat
					1	2
3	4	5	6	7	8	9
10	11	12	13	14	15	16
17	18	19	20	21	22	23
24	25	26	27	28	29	30
31						

November 1926
Sun	Mon	Tue	Wed	Thu	Fri	Sat
	1	2	3	4	5	6
7	8	9	10	11	12	13
14	15	16	17	18	19	20
21	22	23	24	25	26	27
28	29	30				

December 1926
Sun	Mon	Tue	Wed	Thu	Fri	Sat
			1	2	3	4
5	6	7	8	9	10	11
12	13	14	15	16	17	18
19	20	21	22	23	24	25
26	27	28	29	30	31	